HOW TO STUDY

Your

BIBLE

An Introduction

HOW TO STUDY
Your
BIBLE
An Introduction

PETER GREGORY

Remnant
Publications

Coldwater MI 49036
www.remnantpublications.com

Published by
Remnant Publications
649 East Chicago Road
Coldwater MI 49036
517-279-1304
www.remnantpublications.com

Scripture taken from the King James Version.

Edited by Clifford Goldstein
Copy edited by Debi Tesser
Cover designed by David Berthiaume
Text designed by Greg Solie • AltamontGraphics.com

Author assumes full responsibility for the accuracy of all facts and
quotations as cited in this book.

Library of Congress Cataloging-in-Publication Data

Gregory, Peter, 1968-
  How to study your Bible : an introduction / by Peter Gregory.
     p. cm.
  ISBN 978-1-933291-30-7 (alk. paper)
  1. Bible--Study and teaching. I. Title.
  BS600.3.G75 2008
  220.071--dc22
                                    2008023449

08 09 10 11 12 • 5 4 3 2 1

CONTENTS

—— CHAPTER 1 ——
PREPARING TO STUDY

Introduction

I t's one thing to believe in the Bible, to believe that it's the Word of God, to believe that the Lord has revealed Himself to us in it. That's all fine—and important.

However, it's one thing to believe in the Bible, it's quite another to know how to study it, how to read it, how to interpret its message. What good would it do to own a Bible, to believe in it, or even to read it if you don't know how to take from it the message that God has put in it?

Not much good at all, would it? Hence, we will examine this crucial topic: *how to study the Bible.*

First Step of Preparation

Let's begin with the Bible's Old Testament book of Ezra, which reads, "For Ezra had prepared his heart to seek the law of the Lord, and to do it, and to teach in Israel statutes and judgments" (Ezra 7:10).

Notice the process. Ezra's first step was personal preparation; he prepared his heart. Thus, a simple principle right here unfolds; before we seek the law of the Lord, before we study the Bible, before we open the Bible, we should prepare our hearts.

What would be the best way to do that? Pray. Yes, pray. But when we pray before we study the Bible, in regard to what should we pray? What should be the most important aspect in our prayer before we study the Bible? To ask for the anointing of the Holy Spirit, what else?

That's because the Bible, even if written in English or Chinese or Spanish or in anyone's native tongue, is still like a different language. So it needs a translator, and that translator is the Holy Spirit. Only He can truly tell us exactly what the Bible says.

The significant second step in this process is found in Ezra 7:10, as well. Not only did Ezra prepare his heart, but he also wanted to know what it said so that he could "do it." Yes, "do it." That is, do what the Bible tells us to do.

Secular people, atheists, can study the Bible. Some of the most influential biblical scholars in modern history were atheists, agnostics, or skeptics. They knew the Bible inside and out, beginning to end. They could intellectually understand, analyze, and judge the Bible according to their own human experience. But they did not obey it, so they never benefited from the truths revealed in those sacred pages.

Therefore, before we study the Bible, we really have to pray that we will be humble and meek enough to obey what we learn. If we do not have this willingness, then we will very likely be steered in the wrong direction because we will try to twist the Bible's teachings into what we want them to say. Our experience will then be like one of those famous Rorschach ink blot tests—we read into it what we want to read into it.

Our greatest false teacher is ourselves, our unwilling hearts. When we are not willing, when we are not surrendered, when we are not open to do God's will, we will distort God's Word so that it conveniently speaks to the lives we want to lead. It's like the temperature control on an air conditioner; we adjust it to just the right level for our comfort, and then we erroneously say, "Ahh, that's the Word of God I enjoy."

Ezra, therefore, prepared his heart—for what purpose? He sought the law of the Lord, the will of God, to experience it, to do it, and to teach the statutes and ordinances, which is the third step found in Ezra 7:10. Why is it that many people in our church are not teaching the straight message? Why is it that many people do not teach the solid, genuine, most powerful message of Revelation 14's three angels? The simple reason is that these same people do not experience this message for themselves. They do not seek to overcome their tempers and their jealousies; they're not ridding their lives of their frustrations, their pride, their selfishness, and their other character defects. Thus, they cannot preach powerful sermons that would otherwise be theirs to preach. How can they preach, or at least preach with any kind of power, what they haven't experienced for themselves? The fact is they can't.

Motives for Study

Look at this quote from one of my favorite Christian authors, E. G. White. "If you had made God's word your study [if you had made it your study, not just reading material, not just like *Reader's Digest* or *TIME* magazine—your *study*], with a desire to reach the Bible standard and attain to Christian perfection [Christian perfection—we're talking about character, not perfectionism, we're talking about a perfect character like Jesus], you would not have needed the *Testimonies*."[1]

Did you read that? If we had studied the word of God with a heart desirous of living a holy life, we wouldn't need the *Testimonies*. However, the opposite is also true: we need the testimonies because we do not study the Word of God with the desire to obtain the Christian standard and perfection in terms of character.

In speaking to ministers, especially those with very little experience, E. G. White counseled, "They do not themselves dig for truth like hidden treasures, but become careless and satisfied with the research of others."[2]

Furthermore, she wrote, "There is nothing more calculated to strengthen the intellect than a study of the Bible. No other book is so potent to elevate the thoughts, to give vigor to the faculties, as the broad, ennobling truth

---

1   White, E. G., *Testimonies to the Church*, Vol. 5 (Oakland, CA: Pacific Press Publishing Association, 1901), 664.

2   White, E. G., "Wanted, Laborers for the Harvest," *Signs of the Times* (September 7, 1876).

of the Bible. If God's Word were studied as it should be, men would have breadth of mind, nobility of character, that is rarely seen in these times."[3]

What a great promise! Studying the Bible can not only make us smarter and sharper of mind, that study would give us better characters as well. This means, though, that we must be engrossed in studying the Bible—not just reading it, not just memorizing it, not just pulling a bunch of texts together to win an argument. It means studying the Bible with an attitude of faith, humility, and a willingness to obey its commands.

The Bible as Its Own Interpreter

How are we supposed to study the Bible? We want to follow the principle of making the Bible its own expositor. What does that mean? It means what it says—we use the Bible to interpret the Bible. We must learn to understand the Bible from the Bible itself. We let the Bible itself teach us what it means. We use one part of the Bible to explain another part.

That's not saying that there isn't a time and a place to read commentaries, to read what others say about the Bible. Other sources, at times, can be very helpful. Nevertheless, in the end, we need to learn how to study the Bible the "hard" way—learning the Bible only from the Bible itself. We must know what we believe, not be-

---

3 White, E. G., *Lift Him Up* (Hagerstown, MD: Review and Herald Publishing Association, 1988), 111.

cause of what this commentary says, or because of what that teacher says, or because of what this preacher says. We need to know from the Bible itself what we believe and why we believe it. We can find no surer foundation for our faith.

Marking Your Bible

I know some people who like to mark their Bibles. You look at them and they look like coloring books. In one sense, that is good because it shows that they are studying their Bibles. But I think it's better to mark our Bibles in our heads and in our hearts, and highlight the important passages in our brains, in our memories, in our minds.

One way I have learned to "mark" my Bible is when I learn something; I share what I've learned with someone three times—three times! Every time I share it, I also give the reference, the chapter, and the verse. Then I read it exactly as the Bible says. If anyone tries this method three times, he or she will not forget it. If there is no one to listen, then just grab someone, and say, "I know that you're not interested, but just listen to me. You want $5? Just listen to me."

If we don't express what we've learned, it's not ours. If we keep it only in our minds, it will disappear, like a fog. So say it, express it, own it. When we share truth, it returns to us as our own. We must engrave the texts on our hearts and souls. The Scriptures must be written on our foreheads.

Many are so dependent upon their own Bibles, their own specially marked Bibles, that they are lost without them. Marked Bibles appear so holy because they are used so much. They hang all droopy, like an old man. They might be dirty. Favorite chapters may be wrinkled from excessive marking; sometimes the pages are torn and tattered.

Again, it's good that people read their Bibles. I've already mentioned that just reading it isn't enough. Just marking it isn't enough. A life-change must occur.

If the King James Version (KJV) is your main Bible, learn to choose other versions, and be able to teach from them. As much as we may love the KJV, not everyone uses this version, and it's not the version that Paul used. Other versions can be good, too. An opportunity may arise when a marked, personal Bible is unavailable, so another version must be used. What happens if it a Catholic Bible? We might as well be preparing ourselves now to use other versions.

Tips for Learning

"If we would study the Bible diligently and prayerfully every day, we should every day seek some beautiful truth in a new, clear, and forceful light."[4]

Isn't that wonderful? We can learn something new every day, something beautiful every day from this Book.

---

4 White, E. G., *Child Guidance* (Nashville, TN: Southern Publishing Association, 1954), 511.

We can never exhaust its teachings because it deals with eternal and infinite themes. I find that no matter how many times I go back to the Word, I always find something new and fresh in it—new insights, new thoughts, new promises, new challenges.

"If medical students will study the word of God diligently, they will be far better prepared to understand their other studies."[5] (CT 483).

If we're struggling with the topics and subjects in a class, this counsel indicates that diligent Bible study will help us to understand other materials. Enlightenment, it seems, always comes from an earnest study of the Word of God. That makes sense, too, because it is dealing with themes that come directly from the throne of heaven—a little more profound than, say, your latest accounting class.

One time while teaching a class on Bible study, I held up something in my hand and said, "Ladies and gentlemen, what is this? What am I holding in my hand? Did he say plastic? OK. Plastic. Anyone else? Marker. Anyone else? Pen. So now consider this: when he says plastic, it is not the *interpretation*, it's the *description*. So when she says pen, she's getting closer to the main point of

---

5   White, E. G., *Counsels to Parents, Teachers, and Students,* (Mountain View, CA: Pacific Press Publishing Association, 1943), 483.

this object. It's not a fruit; it's not a vegetable; it's not an iPhone. It's a pen. But when he says marker, he is being more specific, and that is the *interpretation*."

My point? When we study the Bible, we need to be able to discern between the description, details, and interpretation. We need to interpret the Bible for what it says, not what we want it to say.

One school of thought says that in reading any text, what matters is not what the author intended but only what the reader reads into it. Some talk about getting rid of the author and the author's intent completely. What that means is that if you have 100 people read a selected chapter in the Bible, 100 different interpretations would be drawn from that one chapter, some radically different, others even contradictory. Maybe that works for Shakespeare or Homer, but for the Bible, for the Word of God—where would be the divine inspiration ion that?

Have you had this experience? You study with someone and they say to you, "You may interpret it that way, but my interpretation is this. Even though yours and mine are contradicting each other, it doesn't really matter. What matters is that we both love Jesus."

That's almost like two people in a room with a table. One person looks at the table and says that he sees an orange; the other person says he sees a toaster. Both are dead wrong, but both of them say that as long as there some kind of interpretation, we will both be happy, and it doesn't really matter what interpretation is. What matters only is that we have our own interpretation, we are happy with it, and that we don't judge the others as right or wrong. It's just different, and different is okay.

No—Scripture does not work that way. No at all!

What is crucial to understand is that interpretation leads to *application.* If one reads a text wrongly, and then seeks to apply it to his or her life, most likely the applications will be as unsound as the interpretation. If the interpretation is wrong, then the usage of that interpretation will be wrong. Interpretation is what something means; application is how we implement it—we should not get the two confused.

Some people focus so much on application that they forget interpretation. For instance, when they read the book of Psalms, they have no idea what's going on in the background; i.e., the historical setting, the theme, who is involved, the author's intent, etc. Instead, they read a text and say, "Hmm, that is so nice; thank you, God" and try to find some way to apply it to their lives.

They can be blessed, for sure, for at least they take the Bible seriously enough to want to apply to their lives. They take it seriously enough to want it to make a change in how they live. And that's good. But many times they can be confused because—without some understanding of the background, the context, the intent of the author— the reader can get lost.

Interpretation, correct interpretation, must come first, then application. We need to know what the Bible says for us to be able to understand its meaning and make it real in our lives. Again, correct interpretation leads to correct application; wrong interpretation triggers a wrong application, and causes a wrong experience.

For instance, suppose someone interprets the death of Jesus for us on the cross like this, "Jesus died for me on the cross; therefore, I am free from the law. This means, then, that I do not have to keep the Ten Commandments." So if, in applying the precept, an individual acquires a lung disease, he or she does see the need to relinquish the idol of tobacco.

No Fast Food Please

When we study the Bible, when we prepare a sermon, it's like cooking. It's like a creating a good meal. Good food requires great preparation. We are not talking about McDonald's, Wendy's, fast food stuff. We're talking about a healthy, tasty gourmet meal. These don't just fall off the kitchen shelf, do they? No, they take work, thought, effort, and the right combination of ingredients.

I had the privilege of tasting Italian spaghetti sauce in Trieste, Italy. I mean *real* Italian food. This lady, she cooked that sauce all day. She didn't open a can of something, throw it on the stove, and voila! Ten minutes later the spaghetti sauce was ready to eat.

There is no miracle in those noodles. Maybe 10 percent of the taste is in the noodle, but the 90 percent of spaghetti's power is in the sauce! Gourmet meals require hours of preparation to prepare and will be eaten in a fraction of the time. If less time is available to prepare a meal, the final product will reveal it for sure.

Have you ever, then, had this experience: a teacher doesn't prepare his presentation of the lesson for the weekly church study serve. Rather, he glances at it the morning he is supposed to teach it, or that's certainly how it seems. How long does he or she spend preparing? Maybe 15 minutes, maybe less. Again, at least that's how it seems. Thus, when he gets up to teach, it tastes like a meal that, needing hours of preparation, was thrown together in 15 minutes.

You get what you cook.

Do not expect fast food; do not expect microwave stuff. Proper and nurturing Bible study takes time just like creating a good meal.

Observing the Bible

So when we ask, "How do we study the Bible?" we should ask, "How do we *observe* the Bible?" Yes, we must learn to observe the Bible. Good observation requires quality time—no fast learning here. In order to observe the Bible, we need to understand a few things: history, author, and context.

Let's start with history, for example. In order to understand the book of Daniel, we need to understand history during Jeremiah's time and history during Isaiah's time. We might ask, "What led up to Daniel and his experience? What occurred before him? What took place after him? What were the events, historical, spiritual, military, that induced the situation in which the characters appear. What was the background in which the author wrote?

Then there's the question of the author. Who wrote the book? Just as an example, we'll use Matthew, Mark, Luke and John. We have four different authors of the gospels, but they wrote about one theme—the life of Christ. But they all had different angles, different emphases.

How do I know? In one instance each of the aforementioned gospel writers wrote a slightly different scenario about the inscription that hung above the head of Jesus when He died on the cross.

Matthew 27: 37 reads, "And set up over His head this accusation written, THIS IS JESUS, KING OF THE JEWS." Notice Mark 15:26, "And the superscription of the accusation was written over, THE KING OF THE JEWS."

See the difference? Why do they write it like that? That really depends on the author. Luke 23:38 says, "And a superscription also was written over Him in letters of Greek, and Latin, and Hebrew, THIS IS THE KING OF THE JEWS." This provides additional information. Why did Matthew forego that information? Why did Mark not say anything about the fact it was written in three languages? Only Luke mentioned that it was written in Greek, Hebrew, and Latin. John wrote "And Pilate wrote a title, and put it on the cross. And the writing was JESUS OF NAZARETH, KING OF THE JEWS" (John 19:19).

None are the same because all had different purposes, different emphases, yet none of them contradicted the others. When we put all four accounts together, we find the full truth. That is how we should study the Bible. One place in the Bible tells one side of the story; other verses shed light from other angles. At times, contradictions seemingly arise, but this is God's way of giving us a fuller and complete picture of what is happening. So when we reflect on the whole Bible, studying one object or subject, we will be able to see the subject not only in more that one dimension, but we will also be able to obtain a full and complete understanding of that topic. "For whatsoever things were written aforetime were written for our learning, that we through patience and comfort of the scriptures might have hope" (Romans 15:4). "Now all these things happened unto them for examples: and they are written for our admonition, upon whom the ends of the world are come" (1 Corinthians 10:11).

We must also examine the context, current setting as we seek to observe the Bible. Let's look at Daniel again. Judah was captured by Babylon; the prophet Ezekiel was in Babylon prophesying; and although captured, Daniel was taken to Babylon to be trained as a wise man. This is the immediate setting of the author, of the story, of the narrative.

Where do we get this information? We pull all that we can from the Bible itself, which must be our primary source although sometimes outside sources can also be quite useful.

As one of the best resources for Bible study, I recommend the E. G. White Study Bible. Before the verses in each book, details about the author and historical setting are given. Even other study Bibles provide background introductions on the surroundings, the theme, and other features. So make use of these guidelines, for they are very helpful.

— Chapter 2 —
Beginning Bible Study

Start with a Single Book

To begin studying on one's own, I recommend selecting a book of the Bible and start studying it. Beginners shouldn't choose Isaiah or Psalms because they have too many chapters. Instead, choose a smaller book. Choose something like Hebrews or Romans, or even smaller: Philippians, Colossians, Ephesians.

Remember, we need to observe the Bible as we study it. Ultimately, we want to interpret God's message for us, but the first stage is to observe. Choose a book in the Bible, and read that book seven times. Why seven? It's just an arbitrary number, I admit, but the point should be clear—we need to read that book again and again to start understanding its meaning.

So what happens when we read it again and again and again? We develop observational skills. When we read the first time, we only have observational antenna one; when we read it a second time, a new perception occurs; a third time another thought will reveal itself.

As we read, we need to start looking for a theme, the big picture. How do we determine what is the big picture? It is a topic, word, phrase that keeps repeating itself. For example, every book in the Bible has a theme, and sometimes it can be described it in one word, or two, or a phrase. If I say, "First Peter," we should be able to tell me the theme of the book like "the details of what a Christians walk should be." If I say "Jude," something close to warning about diluting the pure, Christian doctrine should pop into your head. If I say "Genesis," we might think of the beginnings of history. But this isn't going to happen by osmosis. We must read these books, over and over, so that we will learn them. As time is spent reading, their themes will start coming to light.

Also, in order to understand the themes, we must also understand the conclusions presented. How do we decipher the conclusions? We will discover that the Bible uses words like "finally," "in summary," or "therefore." We need to know the conclusion because so often it is tied directly to the big picture.

When to Study

Another important issue is when to study the Bible. Yes, *when*! Guess what time is the best? As soon as we awaken in the morning. But the condition, the quality of your morning hour, is determined by your activities the previous. If we go to a pizza party for supper, we're going to get up like a pizza. We're not going to have a prime Bible study. So remember that a day does not begin in the morning; it begins in the night, according to the Bible (Genesis 1). The evening and the morning is a day. So what we do in the evening determines, almost, the caliber of next day. Many times we say, "Just for tonight; tomorrow I will be different."

If we want to have a good Bible study, we ought to have a light meal, go to bed early, and search our hearts before we fall asleep because the only way that we will have a desire to study the Bible is when we recognize that we are sinners. We want to sleep as sinners in the bosom of Jesus. Don't sleep all pumped up, like, "I won that game today," "I got an A on that test today," etc. Go to bed aware that only through the grace of God we will arise the next morning.

Another good time to study is immediately after exercising. I like to exercise between 3:30 and 5:00 p.m., when there is a gap of time before supper. After exercising circulation is good, so take a nice shower. We are ready to go when we are fresh and hungry—and because of the hunger, we can think better.

I remember when I used to go to school and had to work a lot too. My favorite work is chopping wood. I would chop wood for four hours every day. And while I chopped wood, I would think about the Bible, and afterward I would go back to my dorm room. After I took a shower, my mind was so clear. It was like a sponge. I was really ready to get into the Word and to learn what God wanted to teach me from the Scriptures.

Yes, when we are fresh and feeling good, our minds are clear—that is the best time to study the Bible.

Last Words

Since we have some background on how to study, and even when, let's look at something else—*why* we should study the Bible.

If you were to write your last words before you die, what would you write? What would your last message to loved ones be?

The apostle Paul knew that he would die a martyr's death. And here, in the Bible, we find his last words, his last letter, "For I am now ready to be offered and the time of my departure is at hand" (2 Timothy 4:6).

And what did he say, he who knew that the "time of my departure" was near? He wrote, "I have fought a good fight, I have finished my course, I have kept the faith" (2 Timothy 4:7).

This Bible text also has many "I's." *I did this, I did that, I did the other thing.*

There is one other Bible text that also has many "I's." In Isaiah 14:13–14, the fallen angel Lucifer said, "I want to ascend unto the most high; I want to be the greatest; I want to be like the most high" (author's paraphrase). *I want this, I want that, I want the other thing.*

Two uses of the first person singular pronoun "I." But when Paul used it, it was holy, sanctified, and just. Paul, by the grace and permission of God, had the right to say "I have done it."

Why? Not because really he had done it, but because he was able to accomplish something through the power of Jesus Christ.

The Fight of Faith

How many of us can say, with Paul, that "I have fought a good fight"? The Christian life is not a passive; it is not just relaxing; it's not just peaceful. No, the Christian life is full of violence.

Violence?

Well, what did we just read? What had Paul written about his life? He talked about fighting. "I have *fought* a good *fight.*" Thus, we have to learn how to fight. It's aggressive warfare.

Some people think the Christian life should be sitting under a coconut tree, drinking orange juice, and feeling the ocean breeze. That might be what heaven will be like, and we might from time to time enjoy that here and now on earth. But as long as we are living in this world, we need to learn to fight every day. We need to get stronger and stronger every day in order to fight the daily fight of faith.

"I have fought a good fight," Paul wrote. How many of us could say that if we were to die today? And then he says, "I have finished my course." *What God has called me to do, the will of God for my life, His destiny, His specific ministry for me to do—I have finished it all.*

What a testimony! Right now, if the Lord were to come and ask us about how much of His work we have finished, what would we say? *Perhaps many of us have not yet begun the work of God in our lives?*

—— CHAPTER 3 ——
PAUL'S MENTORING
OF TIMOTHY

The Young Man Timothy

If only we could, before the time of our departure were at hand, be able to say the same thing as Paul says here in his letter to Timothy. Who was Timothy? He was the Apostle Paul's student—a young minister or ministerial student. Paul kept Timothy under his arm; Paul trained Timothy. Remember the history of Paul in his missionary work? When he established a church in Ephesus, Paul sent Timothy to be part of that church. If we can compare Paul with Moses, we can compare Timothy with Joshua. It was that kind of relationship. Notice, too, that Paul did not write his last words to a church. He didn't say anything to a big congregation. His last words were to a single person, a young, dedicated, and consecrated person.

That's important because God is not just looking for great numbers. He's not looking for just a great multitude. All this has its place. But what this letter, written to one man, says to me is that God is looking for just *one* person—one person at a time.

Let's look more at what he said to this young man because it is so relevant to us today. In 2 Timothy 1:3 he wrote, "I thank God, whom I serve from my forefathers with pure conscience, that without ceasing I have remembrance of thee always in my prayers night and day."

So Paul, with all the great responsibility laid upon him, could say to this one young man, "I have remembered you in my prayer day and night." This shows me the importance of the individual, and how we are to pray for each other, one by one, and by name.

Verse 4 says, "Greatly desiring to see thee, being mindful of thy tears, that I may be filled with joy." Remember that Paul wrote to timothy from his Roman prison cell, where he was soon to be beheaded at Nero's direction. "When I call to remembrance the unfeigned faith which is in thee, which dwelt first in thy grandmother Lois, and thy mother Eunice, and I am persuaded that in thee also" (2 Timothy 1:5).

It is very interesting to note that Paul reminded Timothy of his genealogy, a little bit of his ancestry. Why? It is important to remember our parentage, to remember from where we came. If you have good parents, great; if not, it doesn't matter anymore because you are part of the family of God. But if you do have good parents, you should thank God for them. (And watch out when your mother is praying for you! One reason I am here today is that my mother prayed for me a long time ago. Even when before she walked closely with the Lord, she knew the power of prayer and began to pray for me because I was in such a disturbing state. Prayers of mothers are powerful!).

So basically Paul said, *"Timothy, listen, your mother and grandmother had a great faith, and I believe somehow you have that spiritual DNA in you as well. So, Timothy, don't forget that God has appointed you, He has chosen you for a special work."*

Paul went on to say, in verse 2 Timothy 1:6, "Wherefore I put thee in remembrance that thou stir up the gifts of God which is in thee by the putting on of my hands." Do not misunderstand this text. Does Paul have some kind of spiritual or mystical power from his hands? Like, *Just touch me and you will receive spiritual gifts from on high?*

I was watching a TV evangelist who said, "Just put your hand on the TV screen, and I will heal you from whatever sickness you have. If you believe in Jesus, if you believe in God, just put your hand on the TV, and I will pray for you."

That's not what is going on here with Paul, not at all! Instead, what Paul says, *"I first recognize what God has done for you—for your mother, for your grandmother— and I see the same gifts of God in you. And when I put my hands on you, this is just simply recognizing those gifts. This is a symbolic ceremony to indicate that I recognize the gift of God in you. I see what God has done for you."*

Then Paul continued, "God hath not given us a spirit of fear; but of power, and of love, and of a sound mind. Be not thou therefore ashamed of the testimony of our Lord, nor of me his prisoner: but be thou partaker of the afflictions of the gospel according to the power of God" (2 Timothy 1:7–8).

These words are very powerful. Paul means, *"When you believe in God, by the power of God, you do not have fear. In fact, you have power, love, and a sound mind. We need more of those kinds of people ... and we need people, like you, who are not ashamed of the testimony of Jesus Christ.*

Furthermore, he added, *"And Timothy, don't be ashamed of me; just because I'm in the prison, don't be ashamed. If I can make it more positive, be proud that I am in the prison for the gospel's sake. Or let's put it this way, Timothy, remember why I'm in prison. Likewise, Timothy, be prepared to be in prison, be prepared to be a partaker in the affliction of the gospel."*

Timothy's Charge

Be partakers of the affliction of the gospel. Did you know that when you accept the gospel, there is affliction? The gospel isn't some sort of New Age religion where people sit idly and make noises, like "Ooom," and suddenly have "peace." Accepting the gospel does not mean that no affliction will come near you; no pain will strike you; no suffering will come your way.

Don't turn the Gospel into some kind of peace-loving, new age ecstasy. Yes, there will be inward peace—peace like a river, yes—fountains of joy, yes. But be ready for many afflictions as well.

Paul reminded Timothy to get ready for a good work, a hard work, in the labor of the gospel. In verse 9, Paul continued: "Who hath saved us, and called us with a holy calling, not according to our works, but according to His own purpose and grace, which was given us in Christ Jesus before time began."

In effect, Paul shared with Timothy, *"Hey, Timothy, listen, I'm about to give up my breath, I'm about to sleep in Jesus, I'm about to leave this world, and the work of the gospel is now left in your hands. Now, it's your turn; you must be ready to do the work of the Gospel in the way that I have done it and, perhaps, you'll do an even greater work than I have done. So—get ready Timothy!*

In many ways, we are the spiritual descendants of Paul. Paul is saying to us that in order for us to share and preach the angels' messages, we must have the same type of mentality as Paul and Timothy.

He also told Timothy that God has chosen each them before time began (Jeremiah 1:5). Think about that! What is the calling of God for you? Before He created the world, God had already thought about you. Before the sun, the moon, Mars, Saturn, Earth, and anything that was created, before God said, "Let there be light," the Father, Son, and Holy Spirit sat down and thought about every one of us and had a specific purpose and mission for each of us. And, if we really dissect and analyze our lives, if we fulfill the purpose of God in our lives, we will be happy and satisfied; if we going against that, we will be miserable. We will not have peace.

So in 2 Timothy 1, Paul told Timothy, *"Timothy, get ready. Remember your parents; remember the calling of God for you; and remember I'm about to go away. Remember!"*

Timothy's Future Challenges

In 2 Timothy 2–4, Paul shared with Timothy the problems that he could expect to see in the church. Paul counseled, *"Timothy, this is the kind of problem you will face in the church, and this problem and that problem. And when you face all these problems, this is what you can expect as a minister of the gospel.*

For instance, Paul wrote, "But foolish and unlearned questions avoid, knowing that they do gender strifes" (2 Timothy 2:23). Paul mentioned something about foolish and unlearned questions. Perhaps this is dealing with the intellectual understanding of the truth. Verses 16–18 read, "But shun profane and vain babblings: for they will increase unto more ungodliness. And their word will eat as does a canker: of whom is Hymeneus and Philetus; who concerning the truth have erred, saying the resurrection is past already; and overthrow the faith of some."

Paul is dealing with heresy, doctrinal apostasy. He's saying, *Timothy, in God's church you will confront many winds of doctrines; you will have many people joining the church, and they will say all kinds of foolish things. They will introduce foolish philosophies and knowledge, and they will twist God's word.*

Bear in mind the circumstances with which they dealt at this time. Some instituted the irrational notion that the resurrection had already passed. Can you imagine if the resurrection had already passed, back in those days? That means that if we died today there, would be no resurrection; and the whole gospel is based upon the promise of the resurrection when Jesus comes the second time, right? Thus, we're talking about a serious heresy, are we not?

Don't we have heresies in God's church today? Of course we do. Thus, we need to understand what's happening around us. We have all types of strange doctrines among us today. It's incredible. I'm sad to say that many sincere people become entangled with these strange ideas and false teachings. We have been counseled that there will be three stages of shaking, and the first one will be based on false teachings or heresies.

— CHAPTER 4 —
BUILDING ON PAUL'S
COUNSEL TO TIMOTHY

Solutions

What will be the best way to prevent ourselves from being deceived by these heresies? What did Paul say? He says in verse 2 Timothy 2:15, "Study to show thyself approved unto God."

To whom should we study to show ourselves approved? Not a professor, or a teacher, or pastor, or an elder. We must study ourselves to be approved unto God. That's a high calling, isn't it?

How should we study to show ourselves approved? The same verse says, "A workman who needeth not to be ashamed." We need not to be ashamed. How, then, amid all this, can we keep and maintain our spiritual confidence and courage? In addition, the verse says, "Rightly dividing the word of truth."

"*Rightly* dividing the word of truth"—that means there must be a *wrong* way to divide the word of truth. If we divide the truth in a wrong way, we will be ashamed.

By rightly dividing the word of truth, we need not be ashamed.

Do you remember the message in Ephesus that Paul gave to Timothy and the church? Remember the armor, the shield of faith, the breastplate of righteousness, the helmet of salvation, the shoes ready to give the message of the gospel? Everything makes sense: having the loin girt about with the truth. It all makes sense, except this belt. The helmet of salvation protects your mind; the breastplate of righteousness protects your heart, the shield of faith protects your whole body. And with the sword of the spirit—the word of God—we fight. With the shoes of the gospel of peace, we walk to give the message.

But what about the loins, the belt, why does the belt represent truth? Look at it this way. What happens to our pants if we do not have a belt? They would fall to the ground, and we would be ashamed. When we don't have the belt of truth, we will be ashamed, and we cannot fight. So the Bible says we must rightly divide the word of truth in order not to be ashamed.

How, then, do we fight against doctrinal apostasy? Do we depend upon someone else to set us straight? "Oh, so and so, he knows his Bible;, so and so is a Bible teacher; oh, that pastor, oh, that elder, they can help me through this. I don't understand this new teaching, but my pastor will solve it for me."

No, each one of us should know the Bible for ourselves because when the time comes, we will have to speak for ourselves. Individually, we will be hauled into court. The judge will throw us in jail, or worse, for asking inane questions like, "Your honor, may I get my pastor? Can I give him a call? My lifeline? Can I ask him a few questions?"

That's not how it is going to work. We're going to need to be able to give the answers *on our own*. Can we do that now? What it we were asked to defend, for instance, the Sabbath, what happens when we die, or our church's particular history according to the Scriptures? Do we know how to give biblical and spiritual answers? That's why Paul says, "Study to show thyself approved unto God."

Perilous Times

In 2 Timothy 3:1, Paul wrote about a different aspect, "This know also, that in the last days perilous times shall come." The word *perilous* means "dangerous." What are some of those dangerous things today? Hurricanes? Earthquakes? Weapons of mass destruction? All of these, and more, are dangerous.

So, when Paul said that in the last days it would be dangerous, do you think he was about to explain the wars and rumors of wars, hurricanes, earthquakes and pestilence? No, he did not speak of any of those things.

So, of what danger did he speak? "For men shall be lovers of their own selves" (2 Timothy 3:2). That is the danger that he referenced. When we love ourselves too much, that is dangerous. Talk about weapons of mass destruction—loving ourselves is a weapon of mass destruction.

Paul, though, isn't talking about just anybody. He's talking about church members. He's saying, *"Look, the pagans and the Gentiles, when they love themselves, that's normal. But when church members, when young people in the church, when they love themselves more than God, that's dangerous. They can spend 30 minutes, an hour, two hours, in front of the mirror, but not even five minutes studying the Bible. They can spend $100 or $200 shopping to make themselves look nice in their own eyes, but they do not spend money on mission trips? That's dangerous!*

Paul warned us, *"In the last days, there will be moral apostasy in God's church."* Some young people today come to church, not to seek spiritual things, but to socialize. They view the church as a club, like a YMCA, like a youth club; they spend time with one another, meet boys, meet girls, do this or do that. After the sun sets, they leave for Las Vegas. Some do that even *before* the sun sets.

Paul continued in 2 Timothy 3:2–3, "Covetous, boasters, proud, blasphemers, disobedient to parents, unthankful, unholy, without natural affection, trucebreakers, false accusers, incontinent, fierce, despisers of those that are good."

Despisers of whom? Of those who are good. There will be those who put down spiritual things; those who put down deep, spiritual consecration; those who put down deep spiritual books.

Look at verse four. "Traitors, heady, high-minded, lovers of pleasures more than lovers of God; having a form of godliness, but denying the power thereof—From such turn away."

Next, look at verses six and seven, "For of this sort are they which creep into houses and lead captive silly women laden with sins, led away with divers lusts, ever learning, and never able to come to a knowledge of the truth."

Can you imagine that? That's exactly what's happening with many of our young people. Ever learning? Yes, they attend a lesson study in church each week; they listen to the sermon; they are learning and learning and learning but never are able to come to the knowledge of the truth. That is, they re never able to accept the truth to make it part of their lives.

What should we do? In chapter 2, if and when we have doctrinal apostasy, we must know the trust and proclaim it in meekness and in power. But, in chapter 3, when we have moral apostasy, what shall we do?

Look at 2 Timothy 3:15–17. Notice, once again, Paul reminded Timothy of his history and his background. Paul began this reminder by saying, *"And that from a child thou hast known the Holy Scriptures."*

I'm so glad to be able to speak with young people. Some are about to get married; some don't have any children yet. Those with children, however, need to remember to teach those little ones the Holy Scriptures. We never know if we are raising a little Timothy, a little Paul, a little John the Baptist, or a little Elijah! This also means that we must know the Scriptures to be able to teach them.

The Real Defense

Paul said to Timothy that the Scriptures would be able to make him "wise unto salvation through faith which is in Christ Jesus" (2 Timothy 3:15). Verses 16 and 17 then follow with the solution for moral apostasy, "All scripture is given by inspiration of God, and is profitable for doctrine, reproof [reprove what? sin, moral apostasy], for correction [correct what? Moral apostasy], for instruction in righteousness: that the man of God may be perfect, thoroughly furnished unto all good works."

What was Paul's solution for moral apostasy? The Word of God, and that's because all Scripture is given by the inspiration of God. We use this Bible text many times, don't we? And we use it for what purpose? To prove that the whole Bible is inspired? Yes.

But what was Paul's reason for mentioning this truth? He made the point that the Word of God is inspired because it can change behavior and transform character. God can change a drunken man into to a sober person. God can also change a wife abuser into a loving husband. He can transform a cheater into an honest person.

Be careful, though—when searching for spirituality, be on the watch for counterfeits. There are many. Worldly sentiment has established itself in the church, and it generates a pseudo-spiritual experience that those not wearing the whole armor of god (Ephesians 6:10–20) will think it is the real thing. All kinds of spiritual books are compromised with false teachings, and they make people feel so good. But many do not teach sound doctrine.

Before Paul breathed his last, he expressed, *"Look, there is one thing that I can leave with you, Timothy. One thing that I know will give success to your spiritual life and success to God's church—and that is the Word of God.*

Too many people try to make the Word of God better with *Veggie Tales*, dramas, and puppet shows. They try to make the Word of God better with all kinds of fascinating lights and presentations. But the apostle Paul and the early Christians didn't use those things. They used their own personal experience; that's where the power is. We're trying so hard to show worldly people the love and the truth of the Bible that we bombard them with Hollywood-like lights, neon signs, advertisements, *"Here, Jesus is cool! Here, the Word of God is very fascinating!"*

No. What the world truly needs is to see a genuine faith experience from those who firmly stand on the Rock of salvation. *Once I was lost, but now I'm found. Once I was blind, but now I see. I had this kind of ugly characteristic, but now God has given me better characteristics. I want to be more like Him.*

That's what the world needs to hear—and see!

But yet, we are powerless because we have a form of godliness but no power. What we need is the genuine, solid power of God. How do we get it? By the Bible; the Bible says all Scripture is inspired. And this is the best thing to correct us, reprove us, to encourage us, and to give us hope and power.

I Charge Thee!

In 2 Timothy 4:1–2, Paul wrote, "I charge thee therefore before God." It says, "I charge thee." And the word "therefore" is based upon previous texts, and the previous text says what? "All Scripture is given by inspiration of God … that the man of God may be perfect, thoroughly furnished and unto all good works. I charge thee therefore before God, and the Lord Jesus Christ, who shall judge the quick and the dead at his appearing and his kingdom. Preach the word …"

In essence, Paul conveyed *"Timothy, don't rely on anything else. Only preach God's truth. Preach the Word. Let people know what the Bible says. Just let them know what is written in the Scripture.*

I'm not saying that a sermon has to have 50 Bible texts (although that would be good), but too many sermons do not even *one* Bible text. Preachers share all kinds of stories; they know so many stories from the Internet, and from books like *Chicken Soup* for this soul, and that soul, and every kind of soul.

I've read a few stories from one of those books. Often, they're very nice, very heartwarming, and that's fine, but we need more than chicken soup. We need the word of God. A preacher can share something from *Reader's Digest* or *National Geographic*, which can be very interesting, useful, or fascinating. But what our people need to hear, accept, and experience the Word of God.

What does the Bible say? "Preach the word; be instant in season, out of season" (2 Timothy 4:2).

What does that mean? Well, you know how certain dresses are in season and out of season, in fashion or out of fashion? My own interpretation of those texts is that whether the truth is fashionable or not fashionable, whether it is popular or not popular, keep preaching the truth. Preach the word in season, out of season, anytime, every time.

Also in 2 Timothy 4:2, Paul uses the word "reprove." We all know that we need some reproving messages, and thus we have a church manual. First Timothy reads like a church manual, so that is its theme. But 2 Timothy is a ministerial manual. Paul said, *"Look, Timothy, before you preach, you've got to know the Word in your heart. And, when you preach, you've got to reprove your people."*

That's painful, isn't it? But reprove your people. Then even stronger, he says in that verse to "rebuke" which clearly points to the problem—*reprove, rebuke.*

But, of course, our preachers should not just rip and cut. Paul continued, "Exhort with all long-suffering and doctrine. For the time will come when they will not endure sound doctrine but after their own lusts shall they heap to themselves teachers, having itching ears; and they shall turn away their ears from the truth and shall be turned unto fables. But watch now in all things, endure afflictions" (2 Timothy 4:2–5).

Endure what? You remember in the beginning Paul advised, *"Timothy, you have to be part of the affliction of the gospel. Through the work of an evangelist, make full proof thy ministry."*

The last words of Paul to Timothy—what were they? Word of God, Word of God, Word of God.

You have a doctrinal problem? The Bible. You have a moral problem? The Bible. You don't know what to preach? Just preach the Bible.

A Special Kind of Fast

If we want our church to be revived, we need to revive the studying and the understanding of the Word of God. The challenge is to go on a fast—not a food fast—but a different one.

What is that? Begin by going to the Lord and say, "Lord, I really need to know the Word of God for myself. What am I doing in my life right now that I can replace, a personal activity, with studying the Word of God? Maybe I'm spending too much time in sports; maybe I'm spending too much time with my friends; maybe I'm shopping a lot; or spending to much time online, email, chatting; maybe I'm spending too much time just shopping or eating out. Lord, what am I doing? Convict me to have a certain type of fasting. Is it shopping fasting? Lord, help me."

The devil knows that our church is going to be very powerful if we lift up Jesus in His word. The devil knows it. And this is the very reason why we are always so busy. It seems as if you have no time; it seems as if everything is important. It seems as if you have to keep pace with the speed of the world.

You don't have to!

We need to sacrifice. "Lord, I'm doing something in my life that perhaps I just need to cut away. I want something better. Lord, help me to be able to prove all the doctrines of the Bible, based upon the Bible—without using outside sources, without using other commentaries, just from my own study."

This endeavor takes courage; it takes commitment; it takes a willingness to die to self so that God could be glorified in your life.

The Lord has given us His Word. We need to read it, study it, know it for ourselves. Just as no one can sneeze for you, just as no one can build muscles for you, no one can study it for you as well.

Only you can make the choice in your heart to seek to know the Lord, and His Word. Only you, for yourself, can "study to show thyself approved."

— CHAPTER 5 —
STUDY TO SHOW APPROVAL

Diligent Students

Now, let's look at a well-known quote. "Only those who have been diligent students of the Scriptures and who have received the love of the truth will be shielded from powerful delusions that take the world captive."[6]

How much clearer could it be? In the last days, only those who have been *diligent* students of the Scriptures, who have received the love of the truth, will be shielded from the powerful delusions that take the world captive.

Only those who have been *diligent* students of the Scriptures—not a casual student, not a careless reader, not a surface person. A person who diligently studies the Word of God will be fortified and equipped with the weapons of heaven to fight against the deceptions of the last days.

---

6   White, E. G., *The Great Controversy* (Mountain View, CA: Pacific Press Publishing Association, 1911), 625.

One may say, "I know all the major deceptions. I know about the mark of the beast and when Satan impersonates Christ. That will be the climatic deception of Satan. That will be the final, most powerful weapon to deceive and to entice the whole world under his power, but when that false Christ appears in front of me, I know for sure I will not be deceived."

Guess what? If we have not been studying the Word of God diligently, we will be deluded. It's virtually guaranteed because in the last days, many Sabbath-keeping Christians will keep another day instead of the true Bible Sabbath. Even though they know the truth, they will compromise; they will deceive themselves; they will allow themselves to be ensnared because they were not diligent students of the Scriptures and did not receive the love of the truth.

I like that word "student." I would rather be called a "student" than a "pastor." I want to be forever a "student" because I like learning; I like to learn new things every day. Not just anything new, but new things about the Lord and His truth for us.

So we need to have this mindset that we must become a growing plant, always growing. Thus, I want to show other techniques, other methods that will help to provide a better Bible study.

Sure, techniques are fine and have their role, but if we don't have the Spirit of God, if we don't ask for the Holy

Spirit to teach us with a humble and meek spirit—we will still be deceived. Don't just depend on the technique; depend on the power of the Holy Spirit. Before opening the Bible, pray for the Holy Spirit's guidance because, in the last days, the deceptions will be so strong. How can a person who knows that, when Christ comes back, He's not going to touch the earth; He's not going to go from Jerusalem to Africa—how can that person who knows all that still be deceived? Any of us can be misled because in the last days, the deception will be so strong that we will deny what we believe inside our hearts. In other words, what we see on the outside will be so overpowering, so strong, that it will overcome what we know on the inside.

Thus, we need to depend upon the Word of God alone. When Eve stood before the tree of the knowledge of good and evil, this animal—the serpent, a beautiful animal speaking to her in her language with a beautiful, melodious voice—deceived her even though she knew inside what was right. Her eyes told her, "Wow, this is a beautiful animal;" her ears told her, "Wow, he can speak to me;" and so, when the serpent dropped the fruit into her hand, she touched it. *"I can feel the fruit and I'm not dead."*

Her senses told her that God is a liar. And right then she must have thought, *"The serpent must be right and God wrong."*

Don't be a nominal, casual, superficial Christian. Don't be complacent, like, *"Oh, I'm alright. I'm not going to be deceived; I know the Sabbath. I know pork is really bad. I know drinking coffee is not good for me. I know these sorts of things.*

Knowledge, Understanding, Wisdom

Earlier you read about the various ways of approaching the Bible: observation, interpretation, and application.

In the book of Proverbs, we have these three words: *knowledge, understanding,* and *wisdom.* They all communicate the same idea—mental improvement.

Solomon, when young, asked not for wealth, or power, or authority but for wisdom, understanding, and knowledge. Of course, these three words are comparable, interchangeable. They all mean the same, but if we were to dissect and analyze them, we might understand them in these terms: *Knowledge* is being able to "see what really is." Knowledge is connected to observing, being able to look at something and receiving the information from it—the right information. That's knowledge.

When we see the reasoning in knowledge, then we have understanding, and that understanding is connected to interpretation. It's like, "Oh … this is the meaning of this Bible text." But when we experience, we use our understanding, then we can have what? Wisdom.

A Chinese proverb says, "If you tell me, I'll forget it; if you show me, I may remember; but if you teach me to do it, it's mine forever."

If we hear something only one time, or see it only one time, most likely we'll forget it. But if you continue to witness it, to see an example of it, and to understand it, then we may remember. But when we *experience* for ourselves what we understand, it will be ours—forever.

To a great degree, much of what we learned in university or college has been long forgotten. Even if someone retook the same final exam a week later, he or she would get twice as many questions wrong because even that quickly we forget what we have learned.

In the process of how to study the Bible, we really need to experience what we learn. Then we'll not only know these things in our hearts, but we will also know how to teach what we have learned and experienced. Thus, in the teaching we will know how to draw the truth from the Scriptures in the most beautiful ways, and not just keep the information in our minds. We don't believe in just an intellectual spiritual life; it must be experiential as well.

In short, you have to make it your own.

—— CHAPTER 6 ——
THE TOOLS AND MECHANICS
OF BIBLE STUDIES

Resources

Earlier, we considered what we need to know Scripture: history, author, and current setting.

What are some other materials that can help us to study the Bible? "To the law and to the testimony: if they speak not according to this word, it is because there is no light in them" (Isaiah 8:20). We do have access to inspired authors, but they must be proven with the Scriptures.

When I read other books, even by pioneers of the Christian church, and I don't have any clear indication that that book was inspired, I always read it with a question: *Is this true?* I have to be careful, testing what is written according to scriptural counsel.

We also need a concordance. Strong's, Young's, it doesn't matter. But when purchasing a computer Bible program, the concordance program is usually based on Strong's. A Hebrew-Greek dictionary should also be available for use for when there is a need to understand the original meaning of a word.

I would also recommend the writings of church pioneers, early advent movement writings. Not just any old writings because much corruption came during the late 19th and early 20th centuries. In addition, it is good to collect these old pioneer books by S. N. Haskell, J. N. Andrews, James White, and A. T. Jones, and E. J. Waggoner—very powerful information. Some websites also exist where reprinted early advent pioneer writings are found. These are good. These materials may be used, however, remember that the final authority is the Bible—and the Bible alone.

Another worthy resource, especially from an historical perspective, is the *Seventh-day Adventist Bible Commentary*. It is well written and quite comprehensive. Theologians from many faiths recognize this commentary as a valuable too for broad-spectrum, biblical research.

With access to these resources, whether by printed page, audio versions, or by the Internet, a quality Bible study can be achieved that will rev the spiritual engine of the diligent Bible student.

The Big Picture

I also recommended that a book of the Bible be selected and read again and again. Seven times. Twelve times. Twenty times. However many times it takes for you to know that book in your heart.

As we study and read, for what are we searching? The theme, the big picture—we must see the big picture. There is a big picture depicted in the Bible that takes the whole Bible to reveal it. Genesis has its own big picture; Exodus has its own big picture; Psalms has its own big picture; Isaiah has its own, so do Matthew, Acts, Ephesians and Hebrews. Every book has its own big picture. When the themes of each of the books are assembled, then the big picture of the Bible is made plain.

Through the years of the Dark Ages, God's people were so blinded because they were without the Bible for such a long time. When they read the Bible, they saw certain truths shining through the pages, but they didn't see the big picture. Because they did not see the big picture, God provided the gift of prophecy to help them. By reading these prophetic works as measured by the aforementioned verse (Isaiah 8:20), we can better understand the intention, the motive, the reasons why God inspired the authors to record the words of the Bible—the big picture.

Misinterpreting Texts

One thing we don't want to do is take little texts from here and there, and build a whole theology on them. For instance, some people may try to prove by the Bible that dancing is permitted in church, as if in a disco. Some texts douse the word "dance," but these texts are twisted until the argument is made that it's fine to dance in church.

But when you really look at the big picture, based upon history, based upon the testimony of the Bible as a whole, then we learn that the dance mentioned in the

Bible is not the boogieing, get-down, sensual type of dance. It's totally different.

So we need to understand the Bible based upon the intention that God had in mind when He inspired the authors to write it.

Bottom-up Approach

After we observe the Scriptures, the Bible seems to almost start organizing itself. We see certain images. Most of us know about those computerized pictures; we just look at them, and they look like a repetition of certain patterns and colors. When we look at it cross-eyed or something, then the image pops up.

The Bible is something like that. When we continue looking at studying it and looking at it a certain way, the image just pops up.

Remember those English composition classes? What do you have to generate first? The topic or theme. Then what? You had to create the body. And how did you create it? You had to outline it. Then you had to construct the introduction, the main points, and the conclusion, followed by paragraphs. Within the paragraphs you have to determine your topic sentence and all the sentences supporting that topic sentence.

So when you wrote your English composition, you went from theme, to outline, to paragraphs, to sentences, to individual words. It's basically a top-down approach.

When we read the Bible, we do the opposite. We look at the writing, and we're trying to see the outline, the divisions, the topics, and then the main topic. We study backward.

So we first read it many times in order to uncover the big picture. And then we should read every chapter of every book because every chapter of every book has its own "big picture" that contributes to the overall theme of the Bible. If someone were to say "Second Timothy," we should immediately think of the last words of Paul to Timothy regarding the role or the call of a minister, or we could phrase it, "Preach the Word!"

If you have a doctrinal problem, where are you going to go? If you have a moral apostasy, yet the minister is not doing his work, to which book are you going to turn? That's right, 2 Timothy. It tells you what to do. Thus, ideally, you have to have this kind of understanding and system for every book of the Bible.

Biblical House Cleaning

Some people say that "The Bible is about the love of God." Sure, I say, the Bible is about the love of God. And then I ask them, "What is the theme of Genesis?"

"The love of God," they answer.

"What is the theme of Isaiah?"

"The love of God."

"What is the theme of Haggai?"

"The love of God."

"What is the theme the book of Hebrews?

"The love of God."

Is that the wrong answer? No, it's a good answer, but it may not be the only correct answer. Let me explain. I imagine that most people know what I mean by "hitting the nail on the head." It's so clear; it's so right; it goes in straight; it's just perfect and smooth. But a careless carpenter will hit the nail at the wrong angle, and then what? It gets bent. Then the nail must be straightened before it can be hammered into place correctly..

Sometimes, when I ask people a Bible question, they give me these general answers; it's like they hit the nail on its head, but it's a little bit bent. Yes, it's a good answer, but it's bent. We need a clearer, more precise and specific answer.

When studying the Bible, search for the big picture from the book of the Bible itself, and then find the smaller "big picture" in each chapter of the book. And then every chapter has verses. Group those verses into segments—verses 1–5 is this, verses 6–10 is this, 11–15 is that, and 16–20, and so forth. It is similar to mapping a book using an outline form.

If each book in the Bible is studied like this, then it is studied it in a systematic and organized manner. When a house is in total chaos, and if I ask for a flashlight, then someone must dig through the garage, the closets, drawers, kitchen, bathroom, all over, in order to find that flashlight. But when a house is well organized, and everything is exactly in its place; then that flashlight can be found in a minute.

For many of us, the Bible is like a messy house. We have fragmented information; we have unfinished projects, we have unfinished images. It is total disarray and confusion. If someone were to ask, "Please tell me about this, and this, and this."

"Well, I know, but…"

But if you organize the Bible this way, with every chapter outlined, you will have the answer. It's like using a computer. Don't be fascinated by IBM or Macintosh. Our brains are better than any computer; our brains can do things that no computer can. Scientists have spent billion on artificial intelligence, and still computers cannot do nearly what our minds can.

What you can do is this: have a mental file management program in your brain like *My Documents*. Create a window, and make sure that it has a big recycle bin because we have a lot of things to unlearn.

"Uh, Lord, I'm sorry. Let's delete that one and put it into the recycle bin, and then let's clean out the recycle bin!"

We need to have only a little *My Document* file that says *The Bible*. And when we click that, we see Genesis to Revelation. Click once again and it goes to the big theme; click one more time to find the chapter list. When we click the chapter, there's the outline of the chapter.

Pyramid Power (The Biblical Kind)

It's like having a Bible pyramid—a theme, a sub-theme, and the details; we can have these Bible pyramids filed in our brains.

The Bible is so fascinating. When it is really studied properly, it is astounding to the mind. It's incredible. The intricacies, how delicately everything has been systematically written. Sometimes when I discover something in my Bible study, I sit back, and I feel this chill going down my back. Then I say, "I cannot wait until next Sabbath to share this because this is powerful!"

Somehow God created us in such a way that certain thoughts, certain systems of reasoning, trigger motivation and desire in us, and based on that motivation and desire, we begin to experience a new life in Christ. The Word is so powerful, but it must be presented in a way that it meets our reason and logic and, at the same time, our spiritual nature. And when those two things—our reasoning powers and our spiritual nature—meet, life is touched in a mighty way.

This is one of the reasons why we must preach and teach the Word. In order to preach deep sermons, the Bible must be studied deeply and in the right way.

Thus, we should have every book in the Bible in a pyramid shape, all organized in our minds. Next, you take the framework, the outline of the book of Ephesians for example. Just the framework—the big picture, sub-theme and details, the chapter outlines—and do the same with Philippians. Then line them parallel to one another so they can be compared with each other.

By observing them together, that means both books are seen from one angle, so the parallels between them emerge. The themes and sub-themes match, each one helping explain and answer the other. When we put them together in this fashion—new light begins to shine.

In the next step, add Daniel and Revelation to Ephesians and Philippians, for example—four books at one angle. Add information from those proven inspired writings, a study of the Hebrew and Greek languages; and then history. Put all this together, and a view of wonderful truths of the Bible becomes visible.

With deeper study, avoid becoming Bible-promise-verse Christians. What is that? We know these witty and very wonderful Bible texts, like from Ephesians: "By grace are ye saved through faith." And other Bible texts like, "All things are possible through Christ." Thus, our Bible knowledge is based on these nice promise Bible texts alone. The problem is that we use them only when we're in trouble. And that's fine, but don't we want to aim a little higher and go a little deeper?

What a privilege to have the Word of God. What an even greater privilege to be able to study it and discover for ourselves the deep truths within it.

Five Blind Men

Yes, it is a privilege to be able to study the Bible and to be a teacher of the Word as well because in the end, we all should be teachers of the Word.

That's why it's important to note that the Bible itself also gives us the method of studying the Bible. Look at Isaiah 28:10—"For precept must be upon precept, precept upon precept, line upon line, line upon line, here a little and there a little."

What does that mean? *Precept upon precept. Principle upon principle.* The teachings of God on the teachings of God. Here a little, there a little. The Bible says, *"Study Me this way."*

Five blind men went to a zoo. They'd never experienced an elephant in all their lives; all they could do was touch and feel. So five blind men walked around this elephant and one said, "I know what an elephant is like. It is like a big, long fire hose," he said as he held the elephant's trunk. Another of the blind men said, "An elephant is not like a fire hose, it's like a blanket." He held an ear. The third blind man said, "Like a blanket? That's too soft. An elephant is not like that. It is like a big wall." Leaning against the side of the body, all he could feel was this great mass. The fourth blind man said, "No, an elephant is not like a great wall; that's too flat. The elephant is like a tree trunk." He was hugging, of course, one of the legs. Finally, the last blind man said, "You are all really blind. An elephant is not like a fire hose, or a blanket, or a great wall, or a tree trunk. An elephant is like a snake"—he was grasping its tail.

Who was right? Who was wrong? They were all wrong individually, but if they assembled all of their pictures together into one big picture, they would have been correct.

Let's not have a partial understanding but strive for a *complete* understanding. Look at the whole picture, the whole Bible. We can only do that by knowing all the little pieces and putting them together as a complete whole.

Question-and-Answer Method

At this point, I want to share with you the question-and-answer method of Bible study. This is, I believe, the most powerful way to read the Bible because it will force students to know what they read.

Reflect on Ephesians 1:1. Imagine that the answers are in the verse; all that must be done is to create the right questions. So how is that done? What is the right question? A question that allows the Bible text to answer itself naturally. That's almost too simple, but yet it is profound.

"Paul, an apostle of Jesus Christ by the will of God, to the saints which are in Ephesus, and to the faithful in Christ Jesus."

That's the text. Now ask questions that this Bible text answers. *"Who wrote the book?"*

Now that's a perfectly good question, but this is where sharpening and fine-tuning begin you. In this text it's not that clear, in other words, this text does not mention anything about *epistle* or *book*. So I would not use that word "book." This is being really particular, but it's important to understand because we're trying to stay as close to the Bible as possible. Even though it's not a wrong answer, I'm going to insist that only the Bible to answer the question.

What is another question from the text? *"Who is Paul?"*

Good. And the answer should be, "An apostle of Jesus Christ."

Okay, what are other questions? *"To whom is he writing?"*

Now before we go there, let's digest and analyze this text with one more question.

"How did he, Paul, become an apostle?" And the answer is: "By the will of God."

Next question: *"To whom was he addressing it?"* The answer is: "To the saints which are at Ephesus and to the faithful in Christ Jesus." So basically that's just about anybody and everybody, right?

Because we asked the right questions, now we understand verse one. We know what's in it, and what's not. Did Paul give his address? No. Did he give his mother's name? No. Did he talk about his conversion? No. So we know exactly what is in there, and what is not in there. We must stay with what the Bible says.

Let's study Ephesians 1:2—"Grace be to you, and peace, from God our Father, and our Lord Jesus Christ."

What are some questions based on verse 2? *"Who gives grace and peace?"*

It's very simple. The answer is: "God our Father and the Lord Jesus Christ."

Let's go to verse three, "Blessed be the God and Father of our Lord Jesus Christ, who hath blessed us with all spiritual blessings in heavenly places in Christ."

First of all, let us just understand this phrase, "Blessed be the God and Father of our Lord Jesus Christ." What does that mean? "Praise him," that's what it means. So verse three says, in a sense, "Let us praise

God our Father." Why? We praise God because He has blessed us.

Next question: *"From where are the blessings come?"*

The answer should be from "in heavenly places," and to be more detailed, "in heavenly places in Christ."

"What kind of blessings are they?" Spiritual blessings.

"We should praise God for what reason?" We praise God because He has given us spiritual blessings. *"But where do we find those spiritual blessings?"* In heavenly places. *"In whom?"* In Christ. So we should thank God for spiritual blessings given to us by Christ in heaven.

See what I've done? I've rearranged the concept so I can understand it.

Now, which word or phrase do you think is the topical word or phrase in verse three? The word "bless" or "blessing," right?

What is the main topic? What is the topic sentence? Notice the focal point. We should praise Him for spiritual blessings. The Bible describes where the spiritual blessings are, and in whom they are found. So the Bible emphasizes the spiritual blessings. Simply put, we should praise God for the spiritual blessings.

If we answer that we should praise God, that might be right, but it is aimless and incomplete. We need a reason for the praising, and it's found in the verse: because of the spiritual blessings we have in God.

If we have this understanding, what can we expect in the next verse? Remember Bible texts are linked. We can expect more descriptions of spiritual blessings in connection with why we should praise God.

Verse four begins with the word "according." Do you ever start your sentence like that, just out of nowhere? No, there must be some kind of connection between what came before and what follows, and that must be based on a previous topical word or phrase. What is that? In this case, the topic is "spiritual blessing."

Let's continue with verse four: "According as He hath chosen us in him before the foundation of the world, that we should be holy and without blame before Him in love."

Ask some questions based upon the verse.

"Who hath chosen us?" He, the Father, has chosen us.

But the next question gets interesting. *"When did He choose us?"* He chose us before the foundation of the world.

"Why did He chosen us? For what purpose?" He chose us so "that we might be holy and blameless before Him in love."

So, based upon verse four, *"what does it mean to be chosen?"* In the context here, it means "to be holy and without blame."

Here we have a *development* of truth. First of all, we should praise God, but *"for what reason?"* God has given us spiritual blessings. *"Through whom?"* Through Jesus. *"Where?"* In heavenly places. Take careful notice, verse three didn't tell us exactly what those spiritual blessings are; it only told us where they are and in whom to find them. Thus, we should expect more explanation on the spiritual blessings in the following text.

And it says in verse four, "According as He has chosen us." Therefore, part of what it means to receive spiritual blessings is that we are chosen. What does this mean, being "chosen"? God has chosen us be holy and blameless.

Verse five begins with the word, "Having." Sentences do not usually begin with the word "having," so the word "having" is really based upon previous texts.

"Having predestinated …" *"What is predestinated?"* It means having been determined beforehand. Do we have this concept "determined beforehand" in verse four? "He has chosen us before the foundation of the world." I am sure that Paul is repeating the same topic, but now he's going to give us more detail.

"Having predestinated us unto the adoption of children by Jesus Christ to himself" (Ephesians 1:5).

So what does it mean to be chosen? We are adopted. When someone adopts a child, the child chosen? Of course. It's not like when you have your own baby—you get what you get, without choice. But with adoption, there is a choice.

Let's analyze this verse. *"We should praise God for what reason?"* God has given us spiritual blessings through Jesus Christ in heavenly places.

"What are the spiritual blessings?" Spiritual blessings stem from the fact that we are being chosen.

"For what reason?" We are to be holy and without blame.

"What does that mean?" We are being adopted as God's children.

Is that clear? All that came from just asking the right questions.

Let's continue with verse five, "According to the good pleasure of His will."

"So of whose will does the verse speak?" God's will is for us to be adopted, and this idea of our adoptions was already predetermined. Moreover, God's idea is that we should be holy and without blame. He chooses us and provides us with spiritual blessings that come from heaven through Jesus.

Deeper Study

What have I done? I went backward. Can you see how this works? What great insights we get from the Bible when we study like this, don't we?

Now, I'm going to jump forward to make a point. We've already seen, in Ephesians 1:4 that we are holy and blameless in Him. So take a look at Ephesians 5:27, "That he might present it to Himself a glorious church, not having spot, or wrinkle, or any such thing; but that it should *be holy and without blemish*" (emphasis added).

If we ask a question based on Ephesians 5:27, the answer is already given in Ephesians 1:4. Or, let's put it this way—according to Ephesians 5:27, God wants His church to be holy and without blemish. This is the purpose of God, and it also means "to be chosen in Him." That's what we learned in chapter one. But "to be chosen" is to receive spiritual blessings. So God wants His church to be glorious because He wants to give His chosen spiritual blessings through Jesus in heavenly places.

Let's return to Ephesians 1:6, "To the praise of the glory of his grace, wherein he hath made us accepted in the beloved."

"What does that mean?" This should be easy now—it means to be adopted, to be "accepted in the beloved."

"What does it mean 'to be accepted in the beloved'?" It means to be His children, to be adopted, to be holy and without blame, to be chosen and to receive spiritual blessings.

See how the Bible teaches us? See how the Bible interprets itself? See how the Bible is connected? When learning to see these connections, learn how to study the Bible, to observe the Bible, to interpret the Bible, and finally, and most importantly, to apply it to our own lives. After all, that's what it's all about anyway, isn't it, applying it to our lives?

Let's go to a familiar chapter, Isaiah 53. Let's start at verse three. "He is despised and rejected of men; a man of sorrows; and acquainted with grief: and we hid as it were our faces from him; he was despised, and we esteemed Him not."

Okay, ask simple questions that this text can answer. Remember, *simplicity* is the key.

"Why did we hide as it were our faces from Him?" Does the Bible text say why we hid our faces from Him? Or is it how He was despised? This Bible text is not that clear *how* we despised Him, but it tells us we *did* despise Him.

Look at where it says that "he is despised and rejected of men, a man of sorrows. *"What does it mean 'he is a man of sorrows?"* He is acquainted with grief, but it's much more than that. He is a man of sorrows because He is despised and rejected.

"Therefore, His grief comes from what experience?" It comes from being despised and rejected.

It's very simple actually, but just keep allowing the Bible to answer itself. Look at the Bible text as if it is an answer, but turn that text into a question. That's all that must be done. Reading the bible in this manner will produce a greater understanding.

Let's study Hebrews 12:1. "Wherefore seeing we also are compassed about with so great a cloud of witnesses, let us lay aside every weight, and sin which doth so easily beset us, and let us run with patience the race that is set before us."

"Why should we lay aside every weight and sin?" Sin snares us. Is that what it says? I don't think so. It says, instead, "Wherefore seeing we also are compassed about with so great a cloud of witnesses." In other words, because we are surrounded with these clouds of witnesses, let us lay aside every sin.

"How should we run?" With patience.

"Because we are surrounded with these witnesses, we should do what?" Lay aside every weight of sin and run.

"Who are these witnesses?" It doesn't tell you, right? But notice the first word in verse one. It begins with "Wherefore." That means that it is based upon the previous chapter. Chapter 11 talks about the hallmarks of faith, starting with Abel. And it goes down the list: Abraham, Noah, Enoch, Jacob, and so forth. We have these clouds of witnesses, and they all lived by faith. Therefore, because these people lived by faith, we should too.

But the life of faith should be laying aside every sin and run with patience. Look at verse two, "Looking unto Jesus the author and finisher of our faith."

Thus, in order for us to run with patience, to live a life of faith, we need to look to Jesus. *"Why do we need to look to Jesus?"* He's "the author and finisher" of our faith.

"In what way is He the author and finisher of our faith?" Because "for the joy that was set before Him endured the cross, despising the shame, and has sat down at the right hand of the throne of God" (Hebrews 12:2).

— CHAPTER 7 —
FINAL THOUGHTS

Letting the Word Speak

See how everything fits so nicely together? Remember the text that we read in Isaiah?—"For precept must be upon precept, precept upon precept, line upon line, line upon line, here a little and there a little." That's exactly how it works.

Let's do more. Look at Matthew 5:13, "Ye are the salt of the earth: but if the salt have lost his savor, wherewith shall it be salted? it is thenceforth good for nothing, but to be cast out, and to be trodden under foot of men."

"The Bible says we should be what?" The salt of the earth, and the most important part of salt is its flavor, right? If the salt lost its flavor, it should be cast out and trodden underfoot. That's what it says. This phrase, "cast out and trodden under foot of men," really means to be left under the power of the persecutors. In other words, if a church lost its flavor of righteousness of Christ, it should be rejected and given to the persecutors. That's the interpretation.

"What kind of Christians should we be—tasty people or salty people?" Let's just say that we should be salty people. Remember, though, it's just an image, a metaphor, nothing more.

Predestination, as many interpret it, is a perversion of the Bible. If God chose beforehand that you would be without a salty flavor, that you would be lost, what kind of God would He be? God doesn't say to one person, "Okay, you're a salty" and to some else that he shoe she is not. We make our own choices.

Verse 13 says that we should be the salt of the earth, and then verse 14 says, "Ye are the light of the world."

"Is there any connection between salt and light?" In order for salt to work, you have to have food, and it has to disappear. Salt has to become almost invisible, it has to dissolve; something has to be given away for it to do its job.

"How about light? Is there something like that in light? What is light?" Energy. *"What else?"* In a wicker lamp, as in the days of Jesus, the wick has to be burnt away and oil has to be dissolved as well.

So there's something similar between them. What is it? In order to give something away, taste or light, we must sacrifice of ourselves.

Can you see the similarity there?

Clearly, another way to study the Bible is to keep looking at it and comparing it—line upon line, precept upon precept.

Now look how salt and light are different. When salt is working, it cannot be seen. When light is working, it can be seen. Therefore, we need to be an invisible and visible Christian. Others need to be able to taste our Christian character and to be able to see our good works, so that they may taste and see that God is good.

Look at Matthew 5:14, "Ye are the light of the world. A city that is set on a hill cannot be hid." When Jesus said, "You are the light of the world," He meant that we are each a city, that's what Jesus said. Am I just creating something out of nothing? No, I'm sharing exactly what the Bible says.

A city that is set on a hill cannot be hid. Continue with verse 15, "Neither do men light a candle, and put it under a bushel, but on a candlestick; and it giveth light unto all that are in the house."

I surmise that most people who read this text scan over the phrase, "under a bushel," and simply conclude that it means, *Don't hide your light*. But they never ask, *"What is a bushel?"* Mark 4:21 questions, "Is a candle brought to be put under a bushel, or under your bed?" So many just conclude, fairly enough, that we should not hide our light. And then we continue studying elsewhere, but we must consider and understand the meaning of each word.

"Why did Jesus use the word 'bushel'?" It is used as a unit of measurement.

"Who uses this unit of measurement?" Back in the days of the Bible (this is where sacred history becomes handy), people who dealt in grain used this unit of measurement.

"Who are they?" Farmers or workers.

"So, who uses bushels?" Workers.

And "bed"—*"Who uses a bed?"* People who rest or sleep. Jesus said don't hide your light under a bushel (when you're working) or under a bed (when you're resting). In this world, we have two major types of activities: working or resting. People are either busy making money, or they're just vacationing. They're so busy accomplishing these two tasks that they do not let their lights shine.

Can you see? We need to look deeper. We need to dig deeply below the surface. And when we do, we discover that so much is there!

Summary

We began with how to observe the Bible because we need to see what it says. And then, in studying into the verses, we begin to look at the big picture and to hear their message context—line upon line, precept upon precept.

To reiterate, start with a book, any book, and read it again and again, and acquire the big picture of each book. Then focus the big picture of each chapter, and finally discover the true meaning of each verse, verse by verse, all in context. Let the Bible explain itself; let it interpret itself for you.

This process takes time; it takes prayer; it takes a willingness to not just learn doctrine (however, that is all important), but to let the Bible change you, which is the application that we indicated earlier. We need to go to the Bible with a profound desire to apply its teaching to our lives. If we do this, the Word of God will burn in our souls, it will change our lives, and it will give us a power, a power that only comes from God, a power to teach others what we, ourselves, have received. What's more Christian than that, considering we have been raised to spread the three angels' messages around the world?